72-50

THE PEOPLES OF ISRAEL

THE PEOPLES OF ISRAEL

PHOTOGRAPHY
NICOLAI CANETTI

TEXT
CARL UNDERHILL QUINN

PEEBLES PRESS
New York · London

First Published 1977 by
Peebles Press International, Inc.
10 Columbus Circle, New York, New York 10019

DESIGNED BY NICOLAI CANETTI

© 1977 Peebles Press International, Inc.
ISBN 0-672-52363-9
Library of Congress Catalog Card Number 77-75352

We acknowledge with great gratitude the cooperation of
the Israel Government Tourist Office.

Photographs appearing on pages 2: second row from the top,
center and right; third row, center, 46, 78, 138 courtesy of the
Israel Government Tourist Office.

Distributed by
The Bobbs-Merrill Co., Inc.
4300 West 62nd St., Indianapolis, Indiana 46268, U.S.A.
in the United States and Canada

Barrie & Jenkins
24 Highbury Crescent
London N5 1RX, England
in the U.K., Ireland, Australia, New Zealand and South Africa

Printed and bound in the United States of America

Somewhere in the undatable dawn of Western history there is a tradition about a man from a town in the Near East called Ur of the Chaldees (in present-day Iraq). The man's name was Abram and he was summoned by his God to go out and search for a new homeland. After long years of wandering he finally settled down with his kinsmen in the Land of Canaan (roughly comparable to the area of the state of Israel). According to the Bible his God gave him a promise that his descendants would become a great nation and would have a special mission to bring His name to all mankind. This was the beginning of the idea of monotheism. Abram's mission was not all that clear, and many people still argue about its precise nature, but its importance is emphasized in the Bible when God gives Abram a new name, Abraham, "the Father of a multitude."

Out of this multitude came many families. Today they include all branches of Judaism, Islam and Christianity. This book lays no claim to giving a history of Abraham's descendants. Rather we want to give a portrait in word and picture of a living miracle that exists, many thousands of years later, in the very land he lived in and possessed. A land in which many of his progeny live today. We want to show them as they are, as they live and work together, with their disparities and their similarities, all with a common vision of a peaceful future.

* * *

Since we are writing about the peoples of Israel, it is obviously the pilgrimage of the Jewish people that holds center stage. It is a pilgrimage all too well known to many, and all too little known to others who also claim Abraham as their spiritual ancestor. From the time of the destruction of the Second Temple by the Romans in the year 70 of the Common Era to the Holocaust of the 30's and 40's, it is a story of a people dispersed throughout the world with settlements as far distant as China, India and Nieuw Amsterdam, with intellectual triumphs in cultures as diverse as the Moslem Caliphate of Córdoba in Spain and the Shtetl of Eastern Europe.

A dark cloud seemed always to threaten on the horizon. If there was an opportunity to flourish, there was the ever-present danger of suppression and persecution. People were often compelled to live in segregated areas ("ghettoes") and to wear distinctive garb such as the peaked cap of the Jews of medieval Germany. They were subject to slander, like the "Blood Libels" in Western Europe that resulted in martyrdom for many, along with forced apostasy, particularly in the Iberian peninsula.

By the 16th century, as a result of social restrictions and persecutions, the Jews were compelled to leave the German lands and migrated to the East, giving rise to a new and flourishing culture in what was then the Grand Duchy of Lithuania and later the Russian Empire. They retained both their language and culture, produced a vast literature, both religious and secular, and have preserved this ethnic vitality to our own day.

In the late 15th century the Inquisition began to expel the Jews from Spain. They, too, retained their own Spanish language and specific culture which they brought to more hospitable lands within the Ottoman Empire, settling in North Africa, Egypt, Greece (where a Jewish colony had existed since before the destruction of the Second Temple), Rumania and Turkey. Still others sought refuge elsewhere, in Holland, in the New World, particularly in Brazil and the American colonies.

The dark cloud remained. Anti-Jewish activity persisted in Eastern Europe as well. Pogroms began in Tsarist Russia, the ghetto system continued in other countries, where Jews refused to emigrate. Emancipation was very long in coming, and in many areas it had to wait for the Industrial Revolution of the 19th century and its concomitant prosperity.

Out of the ghettoes rose some Jewish families who through their own genius and good fortune were enabled to achieve great prominence in their respective countries, both in Europe and in the Ottoman Empire, despite prejudice and the many obstacles placed in their way by society. Indeed, some even achieved state recognition by being ennobled (especially in Germany, Austria and England). In the United States the Jewish contribution dates back to colonial times, beginning with the Dutch settlements, and there were Jews who fought side by side with Yankees in the Revolution.

But the horizon was still threatening with subtle prejudice and the unspoken and unimagined fear of what was to come in Hitler's Europe. Possibly the only other historical example of a whole people living in constant fear of having to suffer martyrdom for its own identity is that of the Armenians, who also claim, as Christians, to be the spiritual offspring of Abraham. Franz Werfel, a Jew, immortalized their sufferings in our own century, in his novel *The Forty Days of Musa Dagh.*

Behind the cloud, there was a glimmer of light.

Hope had always been the message of the Scriptures of all the children of Abraham, and in Basel, in 1897, Theodor Herzl, a Viennese journalist, set the stage at this first Zionist Congress for a movement for the reestablishment of a Jewish homeland. It was a hope that had long been fostered in the hearts of Jews everywhere, a hope for a place where pogroms would be impossible, where victims of persecution could finally find peace and build a new life. The Balfour Declaration, presented to Lord Rothschild in 1917, made way for the establishment of that homeland in what was to become the British Mandate of Palestine, a land that for more than 2,000 years has passed from Roman to Byzantine, to Saracen, to Crusader, to Turk, and still remained a Holy Land for all the descendants of Abraham. A remnant Jewish community has remained there from the time before the conquest of Alexander the Great until the present day.

Now the light behind the cloud was beginning to shine brighter. Hope rose in the hearts of all Jews that at last there was a place where there would be an end to persecution, to flight, to exile, to ghettoes, to "having to be different." Immigration to Palestine had begun on a limited scale in the 19th century, particularly from Eastern Europe, but open doors now were beckoning. In 1948, the United Nations recognized a new sovereign country, the state of Israel, *Eretz Israel,* the homeland.

Our book is not only a picture book about Jews who have lived in the Holy Land from time immemorial, or about their brothers and sisters who have come there to escape persecution, or about others who have come to seek happiness with families and friends to live in the miracle of a young nation and to share in its growing pains. It is also about the others who live there and who have also lived there for centuries, the Arabs, both Moslem and Christian, the Druzes, the Samaritans, the small non-Arab Christian communities, and all those who consider *Eretz Israel* as their home.

* * *

Herzl's dream finally became a full-fledged reality with the proclamation of the Republic of Israel on May 14, 1948. The British had left their Mandate and a new era had begun, but all was still not peaceful. The British withdrawal was followed by invasion from neighboring states and comparative peace was not to be achieved until March of the following year. Earlier that same year the first elections were held on the 25th of January, the Knesset (Parliament) was formed, and a Prime Minister was elected, David Ben-Gurion. Although Ben-Gurion was not born in Israel, he came there from Russian Poland in 1906, was exiled by the Turks and went to the United States. There he was active in organizing support for a Jewish state, returned to Palestine and was instrumental in forming a political party and in raising the consciousness of Jews both in Israel and abroad. Under his leadership Israel joined the family of nations and as an already recognized sovereign state she was admitted to the United Nations on May 11, 1949.

Our readers will be familiar with the history of the nation since that time with her heroic struggle for survival as a true homeland, a struggle that has continued to involve victory and setback, internal strife and external threat, a struggle that could be described as the birth pangs and the growing pains of a new nation, founded upon hope, prayer and the fortitude of a people. As of this writing, the future is still clouded.

* * *

As we have mentioned, the country is made up of many different peoples from even more diverse backgrounds. The Jews themselves come from Western Europe and America, from Eastern Europe and the Soviet Union, from North Africa and Yemen, from India and Oceania, from South Africa and South America, many to escape repression, many to find a homeland and rediscover a peoplehood (as Martin Buber so beautifully said), many too to seek their fortune. The cultures that exist there, apart from their unity in Biblical and to a lesser extent Talmudic tradition, are as varied and colorful as their origins. By and large Tel Aviv (a new city and a minor miracle in itself) is a European city, with European (or American) tastes and European culture. In other areas of the country you will find the traditions of Central Asia, the land of Genghis Khan and Tamurlane, or the craftsmanship of the dark Jews from Yemen on the southern tip of the Arabian peninsula. And there are those who have pioneered on the collective farms *(kibbutzim)*, renewing the land and bringing forth fruit where none had grown for centuries. Some of these communities are founded on the deepest of Biblical and traditional principles, while others are quite secular and nonreligious. Yet all have one common purpose, to make out of the hope and the dream of *Eretz Israel* a permanent reality. As in any country, there are conflicts between individuals of differing backgrounds and political persuasions, but there is the overpowering desire of all Israelis to evolve in a just and equitable society into a multifaceted nation where all the children of Abraham, whoever they are, may live in harmony.

* * *

By the 1970's the population of Israel included some 2,800,000 Jews, 360,000 Moslems, 80,000 Christians (of various backgrounds), 38,000 Druzes and other minorities. The national languages are Hebrew (a simplified and modernized version of the classical language) and Arabic. But Yiddish and Ladino are widely spoken and understood, as well as English, German, Russian and other languages spoken by the various ethnic groups that have enriched the country's population.

The format of our book is to show as many of the varied segments of society that make up the State of Israel as possible, including the many peoples of Jewish origin along with the Moslems, the many Christian sects and those like the Samaritans and the Druzes who belong to independent communities. All have the right to Israeli citizenship, and all are part of the great patchwork that is the *Eretz Israel* of today.

Our visits with the people will, for obvious reasons, begin with the Jewish communities. By liturgical and cultural tradition there has been a division since the Middle Ages between *Sephardim* and *Ashkenazim*, a division which is manifested religiously to the extent that there are two Grand Rabbis, one from each tradition. Roughly half the Jewish population belongs to the Sephardic group and it is with them that we start our visit.

* * *

Since even before the Romans destroyed the Second Temple in Jerusalem, Jews had been emigrating beyond the meager borders of the land of Palestine, beyond the land of Abraham, which had already for centuries been in the hands of non-Jewish conquerors. In the major cities of the then known Western world there were Jewish colonies. In the great metropolis of Alexandria (a Greek-speaking city in Ptolemaic Egypt, where the Greek version of the Hebrew Bible, the *Septuagint*, was translated), at Rome, on the Greek mainland (Salonika, Corinth), in Asia Minor, and in many other areas of what was to become the Roman Empire, there were settlements of Jews. One of the earliest historians of Judaism, Josephus Flavius, a Pharisee, and a controversial figure among the patriots, remains the greatest recorder of Jewish history in the early years of the Common Era. He had won Roman citizenship, while approximately at the same time a Jewish philosopher, Philo of Alexandria, a scion of a prominent Egyptian family, achieved fame as one of the chief interpreters of the Greek philosophers Plato and Pythagoras, attempting to reconcile their thought with that of the Judaism of the time. The diaspora had already become a reality.

* * *

Despite the political pressures on the cultural influence of the Jewish communities, they survived and flourished. But it was perhaps, paradoxically, only through the rise of Islam that Jewish culture was carried to Europe. Great centers of Jewish learning existed in Babylon and Jerusalem, resulting in the two famous Talmudic traditions that were the inheritance of the Jews of Europe. The Jews of Spain followed principally the thought and customs of Babylon, while the Germans and East Europeans more generally looked to Jerusalem. This gave rise to the two distinct groups already mentioned, the *Sephardim* of the Iberian peninsula and the *Ashkenazim* of Germany and the lands to the east.

* * *

After having achieved a very high degree of civilization and culture in Moorish Spain and Portugal, producing one of the greatest of medieval philosophers and rabbis, known both to Jew and Gentile, Maimonides, the Spanish and Portuguese communities came under the cloud of persecution and dispersion.

Every school child remembers that under the flag of the newly united Christian kingdoms of Aragon and Castile, a Genoese sailor set forth to discover America in 1492. But too few are aware that in the same year the Jews of Spain were faced with the alternative of apostasy or exile. Some remained behind, outwardly embracing Christianity, but still retaining their sense of Jewish peoplehood and the observance of the law, only to suffer persecution later at the hands of the Inquisition. Most, however, emigrated to Holland, North Africa, the Near East and even the New World, where conditions were more hospitable. Important communities of Spanish Jews were established in Amsterdam, Constantinople, Salonika, Smyrna and many other areas within the then Moslem world.

The term *Sephardim* comes from the Hebrew word *Sepharad*, found in the 20th verse of the book of the prophet Obadiah. The commentators have traditionally identified *Sepharad* with Spain. Jews who emigrated from this area have retained their Spanish language, which they call Ladino (it is 15th century Spanish with Hebrew, Turkish and other elements), and in ritual and liturgy they have continued the Babylonian tradition.

Today, the term has broadened to include all the Mediterranean Jews, whether or not they were of Spanish culture, who under Moslem rule had followed the leadership of the Babylonian *Geonim* (heads of academies). They adopted the *Sephardi* rite and are considered to be part of that community. This would be the case of the many people who have come to Israel from Morocco, Algeria and Tunisia, with their colorful customs and North African culture.

It is basically the *Sephardi* pronunciation of the Hebrew language (differing in some respects from that of the Ashkenazim) that has become the standard.

* * *

By far the largest percentage of world Jewry belongs to the *Ashkenazi* tradition. Again, the word *Ashkenaz* is found in the Bible, in the geneological table of the descendants of Noah (Genesis 10:3), and from the mid-9th century on was identified by the commentators with Germany. The community originated in the Rhineland in the 10th century (Speyer, Worms, Mainz) and spread westward to France and eastward to the rest of Germany and Bohemia. Their own ritual and liturgical tradition stems from Palestine and the Jerusalem Talmud.

As in the rest of western Europe, persecution intensified in the 16th century and many members of the community moved to the East, settling in Slavic-speaking lands (the Grand Duchy of Lithuania-Poland, White Russia and the Ukraine, including Galicia), where they lived in a tightly knit society quite removed from their Eastern Orthodox and Roman Catholic neighbors. They retained their Franconian German dialect (*Jüdisch* or Yiddish = "Jewish"), which became mixed with many Hebrew and Slavic words, as well as their own particular rites and liturgy (including a special pronunciation of Hebrew that differed from the standard of the *Sephardim* and Eretz Israel). Because of the inbred nature of these communities, confined as they were to the Jewish "Pale," they were able to develop a profound consciousness of their own individuality. A deep sense of identity evolved both in the religious and secular spheres and what had been a folk tradition developed into a highly sophisticated literature. Perhaps the most familiar of the Yiddish writers to Western audiences is Sholem Aleichem, who created the lovable patriarchal character Reb Tevye, immortalized in the musical *Fiddler on the Roof*.

* * *

One of the most important contributions of the Ashkenazim to Jewish religious and cultural life was Hasidism, a pietist religious and social movement that was founded in the "Pale" by Rabbi Israel Eliezer "Baal Shem Tov" in the 18th century. His followers can still be seen today and recognized by their distinctive appearance (the men dress in sober black, wear a hat, side-curls and a beard, and do not wear ties).

Despite externals, the movement's emphasis was on the deeply spiritual, on the importance of the devotion and ecstatic prayer of the masses in contradistinction to the Talmudic learning of a few people. There was a transfer in thought from messianic redemption to personal redemption, which resulted subsequently in a unique social structure in which a charismatic leader, the *Tzaddik*, ruled a highly cohesive group and transmitted his authority to his descendants. Americans will be familiar with at least one of these Hasidic groups, the Lubavitcher, who have their center in Brooklyn and who have attempted to revive Jewish observance of the law both through advertisements in the local papers and through a concerted street campaign with a Hasidic version of the bookmobile.

The Hasidim have their own rites and synagogues and a doctrinal emphasis on "inwardism." There are sparks of life in all men that can be "liberated" through particular devotion in prayer (a kind of worship through bodily movement or corporeality), through worshipping God while engaged in the most mundane of tasks (a rather explosive idea in traditional Judaism) as well as through an emphasis on joy in observing the law and on faith in the *Tzaddik*.

One of the greatest values of this movement is to revive among the Ashkenazic Jews a sense of tradition, or rather a sense of belonging to a people with an ageless tradition, and bring them to a consciousness of their heritage.

* * *

The term *Yishuv* refers to those people who have lived in Israel since before the establishment of the Republic. Sometimes a distinction is made between Jews whose families have been in Eretz Israel for many centuries (the "old" Yishuv) and those who came to the country after 1880 and the rise of the Zionist movement (the "new" Yishuv).

Another, more popular term, *Sabra*, is used in a general sense for anyone born in Israel. It is an Aramaic word meaning "prickly pear" or "cactus," referring to a plant that has a spiny exterior but a tender heart. These plants are sturdy survivors in the desert and thus have become the symbol of those Jews who have been able to grow, survive and thrive in the difficult conditions that accompanied the establishment of the homeland as a viable political reality.

We have been speaking mostly of the Jews of the Diaspora (i.e., those who for one reason or another left their homeland over the centuries and established their own new communities), and this might tend to make us forget that there has been a continuous Hebrew community living in Palestine since the time of Abraham. And even after the return of the people from bondage in Egypt, when other captivities and exiles were forced on them (as in the time of the prophet Jeremiah), there were still followers of the Law of Moses who remained behind.

One of the great centers during Moslem rule of the Yishuv was the town of Safed in Upper Galilee, which became a religious and cultural center of cabalistic mysticism. In the 18th century a number of Hasidim also settled there and some of their descendants still remain.

* * *

In addition to the mainstream Sephardim and Ashkenazim, there are some less easily classifiable minorities, coming mostly from Asia such as the Yemenites and the Bene Israel from India.

In Hebrew, the Yemenite area at the southern end of the Arabian peninsula is called Teiman, and there has been a Jewish presence there probably from the period of the Second Temple. Tradition indicates that there were converts from other cultures over the years (including the Himyarite King, Dhu Nuwās in the 11th century), but the community has been known as a living and vibrant member of the world-wide Jewish fellowship since the Middle Ages.

In 1948 there were some 46,000 Jews in Yemen but almost all left for Israel through the "operation Magic Carpet" air-lift in 1949–1950.

They have become an important part of the new nation to which they have contributed not only their particular culture but also their craftsmanship, especially in the area of silverwork.

The origin of a Jewish presence in India is shrouded in myth and goes back to the early days of the Common Era. The fact that trade existed between Mesopotamia and certain areas of the Indian subcontinent for many centuries is established, and it would be presumed that there were many Jews who were part of that trade and settled in India.

The *Bene Israel* (Sons of Israel) are a community that followed the Mosaic law in an isolated fashion, without any historical contact with other Jewish communities until the 18th and 19th centuries, when Jews from Cochin (in South India) and Mesopotamia helped restore them to fuller fellowship with world Jewry. With the setting up of the state of Israel many felt the call of Zionism. For generations they had served in the British army as well as in other government services (as tradesmen and agriculturalists), and a number had moved from their original settlement south of Bombay to the city itself. They had become quite assimilated and the common language they spoke was Marathi. The census of 1947 records some 24,000 living in various parts of India, but by 1972, 10,000 had emigrated to *Eretz Israel.*

In addition to the Bene Israel and the few European Jews who had settled in India there was another old community (the earliest records date back to the year 1000 of the Common Era). This community existed in Dravidian-speaking South India (Cochin), where there were other communities (Christians) who also traced their origin to the Near East, and depended upon the people of the Mesopotamian region for direction.

According to sources, these Jews were divided into three basic groups, who, probably influenced by the Indian caste system, never intermarried: the "White" Jews, the "Black" Jews and the "Freedmen." Their contact with world Jewry had been maintained, however, and their Jewish consciousness never faulted. By the early 70's, 2,400 had emigrated to Israel.

* * *

As we have mentioned, the Diaspora, for manifold reasons, has spread far and wide, to the extent that there is hardly a place on earth where the Law of Moses in its strict form has not been observed. In the Middle Ages, Jews, like other enterprising peoples, followed the trade routes as far east as China (where only inscriptions and possibly names survive of a once living Mosaic community). But with the rise of the Mongol Empire of Genghis Khan and his successors, Jewish communities were founded and thrived in many areas.

Possibly the most prominent of these was in the fabled city of silver and rugs, Bukhara, in what is now the Soviet Republic of Uzbekistan in the U.S.S.R.

They make up part of the "Yishuv," since emigration to Israel began in 1868. By 1892 they had founded their own quarter in Jerusalem.

But they retained their own distinctive customs and costumes (their synagogues make great use of oriental decorations, and oriental rugs!). Their traditional language was a form of Persian (Tadjiki), combined with Jewish elements, including frequently the use of the Hebrew alphabet.

By 1970 there were some 8,000 Bukharan Jews living in the Homeland.

Brief mention should also be made of the small communities of Karaites that exist in Israel today. Although for various reasons these people have been excluded from the Jewish community at large (they escaped the Holocaust in the Russian Crimea, since in the 19th century they had obtained separate status as non-Jews from the Tsarist government), they are nevertheless a Jewish sect.

They were founded in the early 8th century, and would be the Jewish equivalent of Christian Fundamentalists in that they denied the oral tradition (of the Rabbis and the Talmud) and, at least at the outset, declared the right of every Jew to interpret Scripture as he or she saw fit. It has been suggested that their origin may go back much further in history to the Essene community of Qumrân, before the destruction of the Second Temple.

In the beginning they posed a challenge to standard Judaism and thus had a revitalizing effect, but their movement itself ceased to be a vital force and became crystallized.

* * *

Of the non-Jewish population, the smallest and possibly the most fascinating group is the Samaritans. Though they number little more than 500, they have a continuous history in the land since before 721 B.C.E. They observe their own form of the Mosaic Law, regarding the Torah (the first five books of the Bible) as the only Scripture, and keeping to customs that descend directly from antiquity. They have been separated religiously from the Jews since 432 B.C.E. and the fact of this schism is amply noted in Jesus' parable about the Good Samaritan.

In 721 B.C.E. the Northern Kingdom of the Jews was destroyed and the ten tribes were deported by Sargon of Assyria. However, the Samaritans, who call themselves *Bene Israel* (Sons of Israel) or *Shamerim* (the observant ones, a cognate term to Samaritans), claim to be direct descendants of the tribes of Ephraim and Manasseh, being that part of the Israelite population that remained after the deportation. History inclines toward the fact that Sargon brought heathen immigrants from Mesopotamia to intermarry with these survivors, thus producing a religion and a population that was syncretistic.

Yet Alexander the Great allowed them to build a temple on Mount Gerizim in the 4th century, attesting to their importance as a religious and ethnic entity. That temple was destroyed in 128 B.C.E. but another was built and survived until the year 486 C.E.

Despite their small numbers, they seem still to show signs of vitality. Their centers are at Nablus and Holon (near Tel Aviv), and they still retain their Western Aramaic dialect, a language that has practically died out except as a liturgical language of certain small Christian sects scattered in isolated corners of the Near and Middle East.

* * *

Still small, by comparison to Jews and Moslems, the now mostly Arabic-speaking communities of Christians can lay claim to having lived in the area since the time of Jesus of Nazareth, with a continual history interspersed with persecution and triumph similar to but not parallel with that of the Jews.

Their earliest history is shrouded in a kind of obscurity, since it took almost a century before they completely separated themselves from the Jewish community, and more than three hundred years before they saw their religious observance declared the official religion of the Roman Empire. In the interim both Jew and Christian suffered distrust and persecution from all sides.

With the establishment of an "official Church" came an official structure that included acknowledging the bishop of Jerusalem, a successor of St. James the Less, as one of the patriarchs or supreme bishops in the 6th century C.E. (along with the bishops of Rome, Constantinople, Antioch and Alexandria.) The fact that his See still exists is another minor miracle, in view of what was soon to follow.

Throughout the stormy history of early Christianity with its schisms over dogma and politics, the partriarchate of St. James survived with its faithful, as a loyal observer of Christian Orthodoxy, the religion of the Empire. By this time their language and civilization had become predominantly Greek, although vestiges of a Semitic past remained among some Aramaic-speaking communities.

With the birth and rise of Islam in the 7th century came a new presence in what was once the Roman Province of Palaestina. The Byzantine Empire was beginning to crumble and in the year 638 the Caliph Omar conquered Jerusalem. This brought a new challenge to Christians and Jews and a culture and religion that was to dominate the area for more than 1200 years. Gradually Arabic replaced Greek as the language of the people, although a Christian community continued to exist in what had become a Moslem society.

The history of Eastern Christianity was fraught with schisms and quarrels, but the Church of St. James remained in communion with the Patriarch of Constantinople and remains so today. The descendants of these Christians make up the Arabic-speaking Greek Orthodox Church of Israel and constitute the predominant Christian group.

Over the centuries, for both political and religious reasons, some of these St. James' Christians changed their allegiance to the Pope, although they retained the rites and traditions of the East. They are the Greek Catholics (or Melkites) of today.

The Roman Catholic influence was felt in the Holy Land for a brief time during the tumultuous period of the Crusades, and a Latin Kingdom existed in Jerusalem from 1099 to 1187. The Franciscan Order later was given custody by the Pope over the Christian holy places and still plays a major role in Christian affairs today. There is a Latin Patriarch of Jerusalem who presides over Roman Catholic Christians.

In the 19th century other Christian communities from Western Europe (and from Russia) began to come to Jerusalem to establish centers of pilgrimage, and there are now Anglican and Lutheran churches, as well as the famous Russian Orthodox Church near the Garden of Olives.

Earlier, Armenians and Coptic Christians from Egypt and Ethiopia had already established pilgrimage centers, small monasteries and tiny communities, due to their special relationship with the Ottoman Empire. Remnants of these groups are still present in Israel to this day.

As we have mentioned the Moslems constitute the second largest religio-ethnic group in Israel and they have representation in the Knesset. Like Jews and Christians they look to Jerusalem as their Holy City. In fact, the Mosque of the Dome of the Rock, on the site of Solomon's Temple, is second only to the Ka'ba in Mecca as a sacred shrine in the Moslem religion. It contains a rock where tradition has it Abraham was to sacrifice his son Isaac and where Mohammed ascended into heaven on his famous night journey.

Although they accept the Judeo-Christian scriptures as God-given, and look upon Jews and Christians as "people of the pact" (i. e., worshippers of the one true God), they hold the Holy Qur'an to be the only Sacred Book, and maintain that the prophet Mohammed to whom these scriptures were revealed superseded all other prophets. Revelation ceased with him. There are five pillars or precepts of Moslem belief: the profession of faith ("God is great. There is no other god but God and Mohammed is his Prophet."), prayer (five times a day, announced by the muezzin from the minaret of a mosque), pilgrimage (to Mecca, in particular; the title Hadji refers to a person who has made this pilgrimage), fasting (particularly during the month of Ramadhan), and charity or alms-giving. These precepts are frequently symbolized by an open hand, and often women will wear this symbol, intricately wrought in gold or silver as a sign of religious profession much like the Christian baptismal cross or the Star of David.

The Moslem population is divided between city-dwellers and merchants and the Bedouins who live mainly in the countryside, maintaining a style of life that pre-dates the rise of Islam and differs little from their tribal ancestors of earliest times.

* * *

The last group we might mention is the Druze community, living near Mt. Carmel and in bordering areas like the Golan Heights. They have a shrine to their Prophet Shu'ayb near Hittim in Galilee and, although they are not Moslems, they are an offshoot of the Ismailism of the Fatimids with their own special customs and traditions. They originated in what is now Lebanon and Syria and were rather warlike until the end of the 19th century.

Like the United States, Israel is a melting pot of many different languages, religions and traditions.

The photographs show us many of these peoples, in their worship, their work, their relaxation and their study. We see the old and the young, the rich and the poor, the merchants and the students, the artisans and the peddlers, the kibbutznikim and the scholars. We are face to face with the miracle of a young nation standing resolutely on an ageless tradition.

Shalom!   Sala'am!   Peace!

A shopkeeper is observed . . .

taken by surprise . . .

and discovers a friend.

Two more friends, an Ashkenazi boy and a Sephardi girl.

A soldier on leave. Yes, Israeli women serve in the armed forces.

Sephardim praying at the Wailing Wall.

An actress on a street in Tel Aviv.

Off-duty soldier with friend in Kikar-Atarim, Tel Aviv.

Comings and goings of a member of the Traffic Police in Jerusalem.

A tourist receiving a helpful suggestion from a Sabra in Tel Aviv.

A Hasidic rabbi with two of his students entering the Square of the Western Wall in Jerusalem, the "Wailing Wall."

This cross-section of people from different occupations and differing backgrounds gives us an idea of the rich diversity of the peoples of Israel, a microcosm, in a sense, of the world itself.

Since earliest times, the Near East has placed great emphasis on religion and religious values. Under the Ottomans, for example, religion and ethnic group were synonymous, and religious leaders were also the political representatives of their people.

Modern Israel is a democracy in which all religions have equal respect, equal rights and complete freedom, but for Jews, in religious matters including marriage, the Law of the Torah and Halakhah applies civilly as well.

Praying at the Wall.

A wandering Holy Man.

A Yemenite scholar.

Hasidic children.

A camera-shy boy on his way to Shul.

Hasidim in prayerful study.

Hasidic family in Me'asharim (The 100 Gates).

Hasidic students.

Leaving Me'asharim.

Greek priest and Orthodox rabbi pass each other in Old Jerusalem.

Greek priests on their way to church.

Pilgrims at the Church of the Nativity in Bethlehem.

The entrance to the Church of the Nativity.

Historically, in suffering and persecution, Christian Armenians share much in common with Jews. For many years they have had their own quarter in Jerusalem with their schools and churches, and their own Archbishop.

The Armenian Convent of Surb Hagop (St. James).   Armenian clergyman with service-book before the altar.

Entryway to the Armenian Church in Old Jerusalem.

Coptic clergyman.

Greek priest with icon of the Virgin Mary (Bethlehem).

Light is a sign of faith.

Three young Franciscan Friars in Old Jerusalem.

Blind Moslem Holy Man in Old Jerusalem.

Ritual foot-washing, before entering Islam's second holiest shrine, the Dome of the Rock.

Greek priests with Arab women in Old Jerusalem.

Two Hasidim in Me'asharim.

Hasid in prayer at the Wailing Wall.

Street scene in old Jerusalem.

Two Israeli soldiers hitchhiking in Jerusalem.

Bedouin women in the Sinai desert.

Sabra guide at the Pillars of Solomon in the Negev Desert.
(pages 56–57) At the Wailing Wall.

54

A merchant in the Bukharan street market.   A leader in the Old Bukharan Synagogue in Jerusalem.

58

Outdoor café on Dizengoff Street in Tel Aviv.

A stewardess of Arkia Airlines.

Arab children.

Atarim Square on the Tel Aviv beach.

The beaches in Israel, as in any other land by the sea, serve many purposes: sun-bathing, surfing, sports, ogling, social contact, shell-collecting, scuba-diving, fossil-hunting, etc. But in Israel they also serve a purpose similar to the cafes and bistros of Western Europe, where business meetings are held, deals concluded and friendships sealed. A trip to the beach in Tel Aviv or Elath can be the equivalent of the businessman's lunch in New York.

Beach scene at Tel Aviv.

An Ashkenazi iron-pumper with Sephardi friend . . .

and an admirer.

A couple of sun-worshippers . . .

and a child with his Tembel cap.

The Dan Hotel on the Tel Aviv Riviera.

An Israeli of Italian descent playing cards.

Machismo, Israeli style.

Fashion model on lunch break.

Farewell to the beaches.

Two Sabra girls eating the national summer food of Israel: ice cream.

Sabra guide at Ofira Airport at Sharm-el-Sheikh in the Sinai Desert.

Young off-duty soldier and friends.

A painter in the artist quarters of Safed.

Young Sabra singers.

We have already mentioned the Yemenites and their almost miraculous immigration to the homeland. They now have their own quarter in Jerusalem and they have brought with them their skills and their special customs.

A Yemenite businessman in Old Jerusalem.

Shalom in the Yemenite quarter.

Yemenite silversmiths at work in Tel Aviv.

A North African Israeli family celebrates their son's Bar Mitzvah.

An Arab plowing as in Biblical days.   Coffee-seller in Old Jerusalem, with the traditional finjan (Turkish coffee-maker

As the largest minority in Israel, Arabs play an essential part in the growing country. They contribute their skills and spirit as well as their historical presence, guaranteeing the preservation of the Near Eastern character of the nation, as well as the diversity of modern Israeli life. They are full citizens and participate in government with the assurance of cultural and religious freedom.

The staff of life (pita bread).

Soldiers buying pita.

Arab women of Bethlehem.

Young Arab entrepreneurs, selling camel rides.

Father and son.

A ceramic craftsman with a skeptical onlooker.

Souvenir merchant.

A patriarch.

Christian Arab girls in Bethlehem.

The Via Dolorosa.

Arab children playing in the streets of Old Jerusalem.

The new Israel brings with it the same problems that beset the rest of the world when the old and the new are set in opposition. Conflicts arise not only between different religious or ethnic traditions, but between generations.

Dizengoff Street—the Champs Elysées of Tel Aviv, with its famous shops, sidewalk cafés and beautiful people.

The new elegance on the Tel Aviv Riviera.

Young women of Tel Aviv.

Two Jewish mothers at a sidewalk cafe in Tel Aviv.

Young men, from varying backgrounds, seated at a cafe table.

Members of Tel Aviv's "mi-va-mi" (who's who) at the Cafe Exodus.

Old Jaffa contains beautifully restored houses that only the rich can afford, with an atmosphere similar to an elegant St. Germain-des-Prés or Greenwich Village. It has beautiful shopping arcades, boutiques, art galleries and lively night clubs.

New Jaffa has a serious commercial ambience and craftsmen from all backgrounds
congregate here, creating a heterogeneous feeling. It reflects much of the Near-
Eastern atmosphere with its mainly Bulgarian, Turkish and Arab population.

A Bulgarian furniture restorer in the antiques quarter.

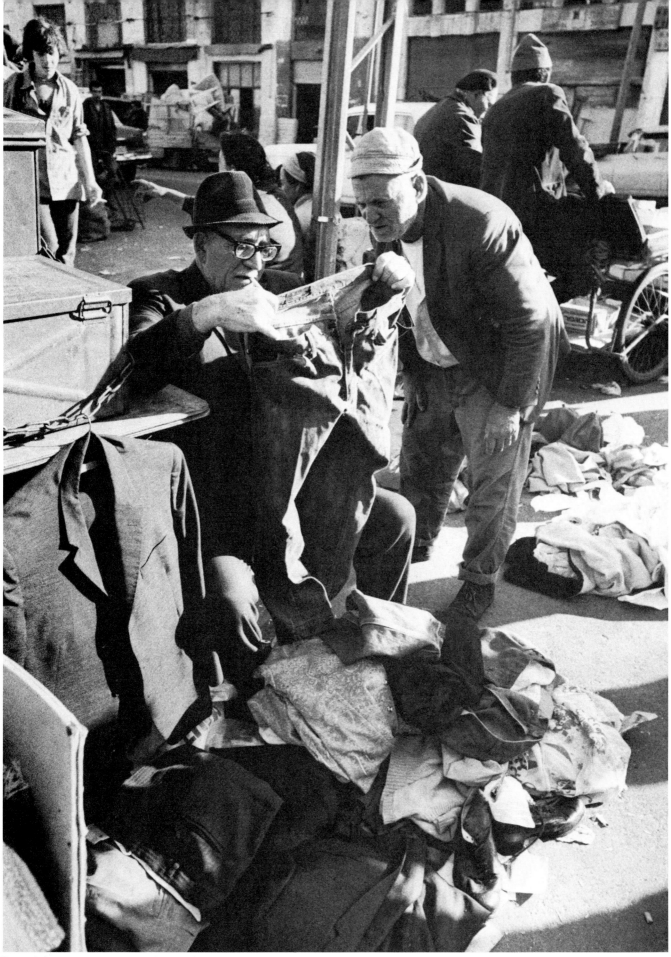

Bargaining over a garment in the flea market.

A disgruntled North African sage . . .

and Macedonian friend with worry beads.

A pita maker and . . .   a pita seller.

Fast-food New Jaffa style . . .   can be found also in Jerusalem.

A Bulgarian merchant on the streets of New Jaffa, and a beggar from the North African Atlas Mountains.

Three generations who have found a home on the Shfa'im Kibbutz. The youngest son at the cow barn . . .

Of all the experiments-in-living in Israel, there is one that is truly unique in the world, the kibbutz. The word itself means "in-gathering," and the concept implies community of production and consumption as well as property that is held in common.

People come together for one common goal, most often agricultural, that is decided upon by the group itself. It can be religion-oriented or even secular, but it always presupposes the creation of a community that is self-sufficient, in which each member works for the common good of all. Superficially it could be compared to the monastic establishments of Western Europe during the Middle Ages, or to the practical outcome of a kind of socialist idealism. But there is a vast difference. The kibbutzim are family communities. Generations work together and each family member has his or her own special task.

The youngest children go to day-care centers (now so common in America), while the older ones study and work according to their schedules. Money is a nonexistent commodity since all goods are shared. Even work-roles change from day to day.

Interested people from everywhere can join a kibbutz. There are no special "contracts," and everyone may come and go as they please. Gifts (and quirks) of individual personality are honored and preserved.

The greening of the Negev desert is one proof of the success in this experiment in living.

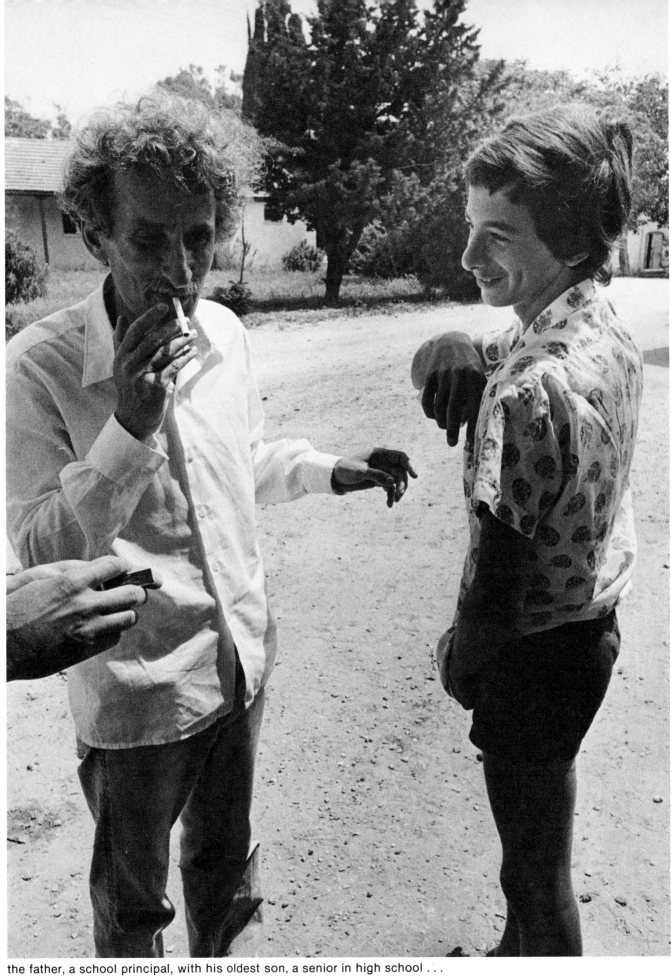

the father, a school principal, with his oldest son, a senior in high school . . .

the pioneer grandfather still at work in the kibbutz's plastic factory...

The youngest daughter enjoying lunch at kindergarten.

Painted toenails and saucy T-shirts, previously banned, are now allowed in the kibbutz.

The Tembel hat again. Everybody works.

124

Dairy farmer.

Kibbutznikit working on a tractor at Eilat, an oasis-Kibbutz in the Negev . . .   and the next day in the kitchen.

Modern milking machines.

But cities and kibbutzim are not all there is to Israel by any means. In addition to the Arab intellectuals, merchant class and city dwellers, there are also the Bedouins, who continue to live as their ancestors did so many generations before them in the desert.

Bedouins at the foot of Sinai desert mountains.

Resting in the sun.

Bedouin child.

A gasoline station in the middle of the desert, run by a Bedouin.

We said that the beach was a meeting place for so many things, but it is also a place for serious sports . . . early morning exercise . . . and late evening jogging.

Sailing—the new "in" sport at the Marina Club in Tel Aviv.   Paddle-ball is the national beach sport.

Water-skiing on the Sea of Galilee and soccer in Acre.

Medicine ball.

Young weightlifters.

Games are also an essential part of the people's life. Here, Bulgarians playing dominoes in Jaffa.

Sheshbesh (backgammon) is very popular.

A leader of the Old Bukharan Synagogue in Jerusalem.

Silversmith and food merchant.

Some of the most interesting Israelis are immigrants from Central Asia, the land of Genghis Khan. They too give vitality to this new nation with their emphasis on their Oriental heritage and their clinging to tradition.

145

Greengrocer at the market in the Bukharan Quarter.

Rumanian women on a lunch break.

For the children of Israel the future holds great promise, the promise first made to Abraham. They live in a land that is free, within the context of a dream that is becoming a reality. They have never really known the suffering and struggle of their parents and grandparents. Yet they too live on the brink of the unknown. The dark cloud on the horizon with its threat of war is never completely absent from the placid security of childhood and the warmth of family life.

Young students on the campus of the Hebrew University of Jerusalem

Actresses in the make-up room on a movie set.

Young girl working in ceramics, a major craft in Israel.

Sabra police woman of North African descent at Ben-Gurion Airport.

Sabra girls.

High school children learning about their country . . .

and, on a break, how to play chess.

Hitchhiking in Elath.

A ground crewman on duty.

Stewardess from Arkia, the domestic airline.

The "now" generation at leisure and at work . . .

There is always the sea and its mysteries.

Children playing on a sculpture by Henry Moore.

Tears in Tel Aviv.

A new generation is playing in the newly reconstructed Jewish Quarter in Jerusalem.

Children at the Israel Museum and . . . at the F. Mann Cultural Center.

Sephardi twins.

Parents and children in the streets of Israel.

There is an essential aspect of Israeli life that is not always obvious. In the Bible it was the patriarchs who always seemed to be in the limelight, and on a cursory reading of the book, it is easy to conclude that women and mothers were relegated most often to second place. Think, for example, of what happened to Eve and to Lot's wife! But we have also to remember Ruth and Naomi, Deborah and Judith, Sarah and Rebekah, and of course, Queen Esther. And this is without even speaking of the Christian and Moslem reverence for Mary, the Mother of Jesus. (An entire surah of the Qur'an is devoted to her!)

In the preceding pages we have had a few tiny glimpses of Israeli family life and the close relationship between mother and child. The proverbial "Jewish mother" has kept the family together for centuries, and in fact it is she and not her husband who passes on "Jewishness" to her child. In a very vital way, it is the mother, with her love and dedication, who is the future of Israel today.